# A Note to Parents

DK READERS is a compelling program for beginning readers, designed in conjunction with leading literacy experts, including Dr. Linda Gambrell, Distinguished Professor of Education at Clemson University. Dr. Gambrell has served as President of the National Reading Conference, the College Reading Association, and the International Reading Association.

Beautiful illustrations and superb full-color photographs combine with engaging, easy-to-read stories to offer a fresh approach to each subject in the series. Each DK READER is guaranteed to capture a child's interest while developing his or her reading skills, general knowledge, and love of reading.

The five levels of DK READERS are aimed at different reading abilities, enabling you to choose the books that are exactly right for your child:

**Pre-level 1:** Learning to read
**Level 1:** Beginning to read
**Level 2:** Beginning to read alone
**Level 3:** Reading alone
**Level 4:** Proficient readers

The "normal" age at which a child begins to read can be anywhere from three to eight years old. Adult participation through the lower levels is very helpful for providing encouragement, discussing storylines, and sounding out unfamiliar words.

No matter which level you select, you can be sure that you are helping your child learn to read, then read to learn!

LONDON, NEW YORK, MUNICH,
MELBOURNE, AND DELHI

**Written by** Fiona Lock

**Series Editor** Deborah Lock
**U.S. Editor** John Searcy
**Project Art Editor** Mary Sandberg
**Production Editor** Siu Yin Chan
**Production** Claire Pearson
**Jacket Designer** Mary Sandberg

**Reading Consultant**
Linda Gambrell, Ph.D.

First American Edition, 2009
13 10 9
Published in the United States by DK Publishing
345 Hudson Street, New York, New York 10014
008-DD503-Mar/2009
Copyright © 2009 Dorling Kindersley Limited

DK books are available at special discounts when purchased in bulk for sales
promotions, premiums, fund-raising, or educational use.
For details, contact:
DK Publishing Special Markets
345 Hudson Street
New York, New York 10014
SpecialSales@dk.com

A catalog record for this book
is available from the Library of Congress
ISBN: 978-0-7566-4295-2 (Paperback)
ISBN: 978-0-7566-4294-5 (Hardcover)

Color reproduction by Colourscan, Singapore
Printed and bound in China by L Rex Printing Co., Ltd.

The publisher would like to thank Elizabeth Bartlett
as equestrian consultant.
The publisher would also like to thank the following for their kind
permission to reproduce their photographs:
a=above; b=below; c=center; l=left; r=right; t=top
**Alamy Images:** Tim Graham 20-21; Peter Llewellyn 17c; Lourens
Smak 15tr. **Corbis:** Walter Bieri / EPA 22t; Christopher Cormack 27t;
Ariel Skelley 7t. **DK Images:** Mr. and Mrs. Dimmock 8br, 9bc; John
Goddard Fenwick and Lyn Moran 22bl; Haras National de Compiegne,
France 19bc; Miss. H Houlden 7bl, 7fbr; Stephen Oliver 6c, 16br, 17bc,
21br, 21fbl; Stephen Oliver / Courtesy of Sally Chaplin 29br, 29fbl;
Darwin Olsen, Kentucky Horse Park, USA 8bl, 9bl, 9fbr; Pegasus
Stables, Newmarket 24br, 25bl. **FLPA:** Gerard Lacz 18-19, 30bl. **Getty
Images:** Gallo Images / Travel Ink 4-5. **Masterfile:** R. Ian Lloyd 28-29.
**Photolibrary:** Creatas 12-13. **Shutterstock:** Condor 36 31br; Dennis
Donohue 24-25; Kondrashov MIkhail Evgenevich 16t. **Still Pictures:**
Biosphoto / Klein J.-L. & Hubert M.-L. 14-15. **SuperStock:**
Age Fotostock 30-31.
**Jacket images Front: Getty Images:** National Geographic /
Ralph Lee Hopkins.
All other images © Dorling Kindersley
For further information see: www.dkimages.com

Discover more at
**www.dk.com**

# Contents

**DK** READERS

LEARNING
pre-level
**1**
TO READ

# Ponies and Horses

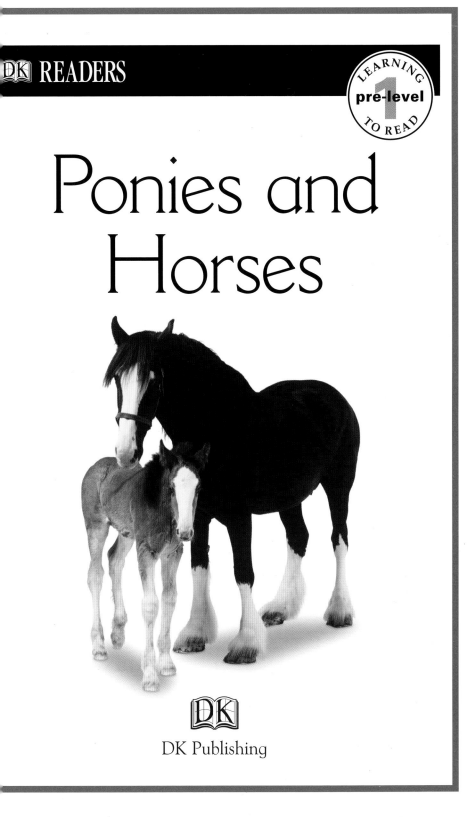

DK
DK Publishing

Welcome to
the stable yard.
The horses are
eating and drinking.

hay

# The pony has to be brushed and washed.

brush

grooming kit

brown horses

The brown horse
has horseshoes
fitted to its hooves.

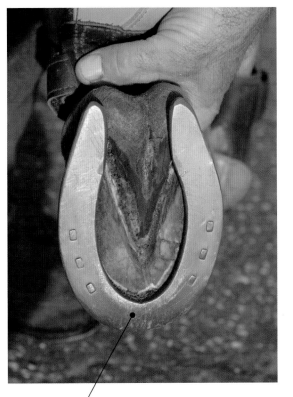

horseshoe

The rider puts a saddle on the palomino [pal-uh-MEE-no] pony.

saddle

palomino ponies

The chestnut horses
go for a walk.
The riders wear
riding hats.

chestnut horses

riding hat

bridle

13

The horse and its foal graze in the field.

foals

foal

black horses

People watch
the black horses at
the horse show.

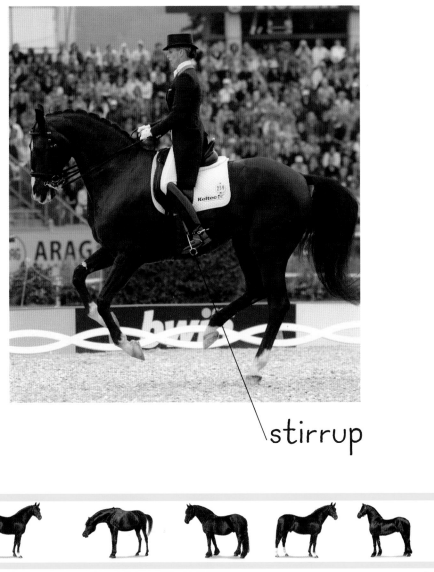

stirrup

The rider tells
the gray pony to trot
and then to canter.

 gray ponies

rider

The bay horse jumps over the fence.

fence

bay horses

dancing horses

The dancing horses
jump and
leap.

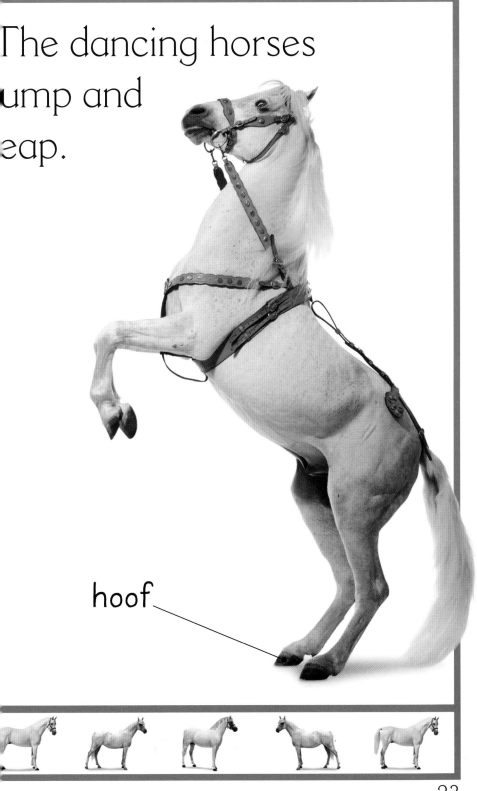

hoof

jockey

racehorses

The racehorses race around the track. Who will win?

track

polo stick

polo ponies

The polo ponies
run up and down
the polo field.

Cowboys ride
ranch horses to
round up the cattle.

 ranch horses

cowboy

cattle

The wild horses gallop across a river.

Can you gallop

like a horse?

# Glossary

**Brush** a tool for brushing the hair of a horse

**Fence** a row of bars for a horse to jump over

**Hooves** the feet of a horse

**Riding hat** a hard hat that a horse rider wears

**Saddle** a seat for a rider that is tied onto a horse's back